Leading for Results

Leading for Results

Five Practices to Use in Your
Personal and Professional Life

Distilled from Twenty-Five Years of
Teaching Leadership around the World

JOAN BRAGAR, EDD

BOSTON CENTER FOR LEADERSHIP DEVELOPMENT

LEADING FOR RESULTS
FIVE PRACTICES TO USE IN YOUR PERSONAL
AND PROFESSIONAL LIFE

iUniverse books may be ordered through booksellers or by contacting:

iUniverse
1663 Liberty Drive
Bloomington, IN 47403
www.iuniverse.com
1-800-Authors (1-800-288-4677)

ISBN: 978-1-4917-8058-9 (sc)
ISBN: 978-1-4917-8059-6 (e)

Print information available on the last page.

iUniverse rev. date: 12/3/2015

Dedicated to the memory of my father, Norman Bragar, who taught me, *"You don't manage people, you lead them."*

I would like to acknowledge the many people with whom I have learned the art and practice of leadership, but the list is far too long. This book is filled with references to outstanding teachers, clients, colleagues, students, friends, and relatives. You have each contributed immeasurably to my understanding, and I am deeply grateful to you.

To my longtime editor and friend Kathleen Lancaster, whose steadfast critical encouragement supported this book's emergence —thank you for bringing clarity and structure to my work.

Contents

Introduction

Whatever you can do, or believe you can, begin it.
Boldness has genius power and magic in it!
—Attributed to Goethe in William Hutchinson
Murray, *The Scottish Himalayan Expedition*

Is there something you care deeply about accomplishing? Will
you need to lead others to achieve this outcome? Whether or not
you currently think of yourself as a leader, would you benefit from
learning how to influence others to work with you in achieving
the results you have envisioned? If so, this book is for you.

This is not a book about the lives of famous leaders, nor is it an
academic book with multiple theories of leadership. Instead, this
is a book about *leading*, which I define as "empowering ourselves
and others to face challenges and achieve results."

It is a practical guide that presents, clearly and simply, five
essential practices you can use to lead others to accomplish the
results you most care about. I have distilled these practices from
the best thinking in the field of leadership development, refined
through my own research and experience in teaching people to
lead in organizations, communities, and universities around the

world. The thousands of people who have used these practices to transform their abilities to lead others for results have shown that these practices are both effective and simple to apply.

This book makes the practices of *Leading for Results* available to readers who may not have access to a leadership development program but are eager to learn how to achieve great results on the issues that they most care about. Each chapter explains a practice and then illustrates it with examples from the leadership development programs that I have designed and led. At the end of each chapter there are exercises for you to perform and apply to your own leadership challenges.

As we apply the practices, we learn to shift our awareness about our impact in the world. We move from feeling that "the world is happening to me" to a perception that "I am happening to the world." This shift occurs through the process of seeing clearly a future that we want to create, involving others in analyzing the obstacles, and then committing to the actions needed to bring that future into reality. In simple terms, you may use these practices as a way of knowing where you want to go and what you have to do to overcome what's in the way of getting there.

The five practices for leading for results are:

- Knowing your purpose

- Envisioning a better future

- Clarifying your challenge

- Aligning your stakeholders

- Learning and adapting to change

Notice that these practices are all named using *gerunds*—verb-based nouns ending in *"ing"* that express ongoing actions. As such they show that leading is a continuously evolving process. We don't come once and for all to *know* our purpose. We are continually becoming aware of *knowing* what our purpose is. Similarly, we don't *adapt* to change once and for all. To be effective we are constantly *adapting* to change.

I learned the value of *practices*, or "sets of behaviors that contribute to an outcome," as a way of teaching leadership development while working at the global business-training firm the Forum Corporation, headquartered in Boston. In my work there I researched and validated the practices of high-performing managers when they were most effective at leading and influencing others.

This research became the basis of my doctoral dissertation at Harvard: "Effective Leadership Practices for Managers: Balancing Interdependence and Autonomy." For the past thirty years I have used these practices in designing leadership programs for two arenas: global multinational corporations and public health ministries in some of the poorest countries in the world. This book explains how to apply these practices to your own challenges.

LEARNING FROM COMMITTED PEOPLE
FROM AROUND THE WORLD

In my work with business managers in industrialized countries and health managers in impoverished countries, I have been struck by the extraordinary commitment and resourcefulness that people draw on to improve their conditions, even in the most difficult of circumstances. You will find stories drawn from many of these experiences in this book.

The practices have been proven effective, not only in leading others to achieve results, but also in enabling individuals to *lead their lives*. To illustrate this, I include a chapter from my own life. A few years ago I was a passenger on a small plane that crash-landed during a flight over central Massachusetts. I needed to use all of these practices to put myself back on my feet. You can read about my long recovery from the injuries of this crash and what I learned about the power of recommitting to my purpose and vision in that chapter.

ON TO THE PRACTICES!

If you have read this far, and you are interested in learning how to lead for results, I am confident that you will benefit from the practices explained in this book. I've witnessed people in countries from Afghanistan to Tanzania, who, with few resources other than their hearts and their minds, have learned to lead. I have found again and again that when people have a clear image of what they want to achieve, and have a process for overcoming the obstacles they face, they can achieve results far beyond their expectations.

I invite you to use these practices to manifest your own purpose and change the world for the better, one result at a time.

Practice One:
Knowing Your Purpose

This is the true joy of life—being used for a purpose
recognized by yourself as a mighty one.
—George Bernard Shaw

- *The benefits of knowing your purpose*

- *Aligning your purpose with others*

- *Discovering your purpose*

Knowing your purpose—what you are uniquely here to contribute—is at the heart of achieving the results you want. One of my teachers, Peter Senge, put it this way in a recent dialogue with colleagues: "Everyone has a unique intentionality that we're born with. We need to keep cultivating and nurturing that."

I use the word *purpose* in a way similar to the way the word *mission* is used in organizations. A mission statement defines why an organization exists, its reason for being. When working with others you need to identify and state your group's shared purpose. You ask at the beginning of your work together, "Why are we here-what is the purpose of this group or meeting?" You then use this mission to guide your decisions and actions.

A clear personal purpose statement will express what you, as an individual, are uniquely contributing. Identifying your purpose may at first feel like a somewhat overwhelming activity, but I have found that it is possible to do this through a series of reflections. Once you have crafted a purpose statement that reflects your true aspirations, your path becomes clearer, and opportunities and resources open up that would not have appeared before.

I have discovered that my own purpose is "to teach leadership to high-performers who want to make a difference." These high-performers could be health workers, engineers, or artists. What they have in common is their commitment to excellence and contribution to others. Knowing this purpose gives clarity to my activities and choices. It is the reason I do all of my work, and it enables me to live a life of contribution myself. I know not to get involved in work that does not reflect this purpose. Therefore, I focus my work on clients and students who are high-performers who want to make a difference.

Knowing my purpose has given me the clarity of mind to focus my education, training, and professional choices. It has also impacted the personal choices I made, including the values I emphasized when I was raising my children.

Your purpose may already be evident in your life. Most of us are already living lives that bear some relationship to our purpose. Usually, however, we don't take the time to reflect fully on what has led us to this place, or to clarify in words the purpose that underlies the choices we have made. For example, my daughter, Rebecca Rondeau, was very caring about her friends when she was in college, and was always ready to support them when they had a problem, even if it took away from her own study time. At first

I thought this was detracting from her learning, so I would urge her to pay more attention to her schoolwork.

But as I saw her purpose emerging, her priorities began to make sense. She was drawn to human service, and as she began to focus her studies in that area, she became a more satisfied and better student. She eventually became a clinical social worker, a child and family therapist who spends her days listening compassionately to others in need both in her work and with her family. Living in harmony with her purpose fulfills her life.

THE BENEFITS OF KNOWING YOUR PURPOSE

When you clarify your purpose, you will find that you have a better understanding of the choices you make. Your decisions, both conscious and unconscious, will begin to operate in alignment with your purpose. The actions you take will become more focused and effective. And this clarity will affect the people around you, who will be inspired to support you.

When I introduce the idea of purpose in a work setting, I invite people to take time to reflect on the question: What are we really trying to do? The story below illustrates how this works.

STORY: CLARIFYING THE PURPOSE OF AN ADVERTISING AGENCY

I worked with the leadership team of an innovative Boston-based advertising agency, aptly named Small Army, which was trying to work in a way that reflected their social conscience. One way they did this was by founding a nonprofit organization to raise money for cancer research.

When the team members reflected on what truly inspired them in their work—what was a greater calling for them than just making money—they discovered that what they cared deeply about was telling their clients' stories in a way that communicated values and moved people to act.

The leadership team clarified that their purpose was "to partner with confident brands to tell amazing stories that move people to act." They inscribed the moral of their own story on the wall of their agency: "The strongest relationships are built on shared beliefs."

Once they were clear on their purpose, they found that they were better able to communicate what they were trying to do, both with clients and with their colleagues. And more importantly, they were better able to attract clients who were aligned with their company's values.

> **Reflection—Ask yourself:**
>
> • *What truly inspires me?*
>
> • *How does this reflect what I most deeply care about?*
>
> • *Begin to write down some words to use in a draft purpose statement.*

ALIGNING YOUR PURPOSE WITH OTHERS'

The power of clarifying your purpose and aligning it with other people's purposes is illustrated in the following story of how the Leadership Development Program (LDP) in international public health was launched. Throughout the story, you will see how aligning many stakeholders' purposes, including my own, and those of the health managers in Egypt, launched and sustained this important program.

STORY: ALIGNING PURPOSES TO IMPROVE HEALTH CARE IN RURAL EGYPT

In February 2002, I was working as Director of Leadership Development with Management Sciences for Health (MSH), a global nonprofit organization whose mission is "to save lives and improve the health of the world's poorest and most vulnerable people by closing the gap between knowledge and action in public health."

I was invited to Egypt to give a keynote speech at a conference for ministries of health from the Middle East about the leadership practices used by high-performing public health leaders. My plan was to make the speech, see the pyramids, and return home to Boston.

That plan got waylaid. After my speech, Dr. Morsi Mansour, a surgeon and senior manager from the Egypt Ministry of Health and Population, approached me. His purpose, which we later discovered, was "to empower the front line of health workers." He invited me to stay in Egypt to conduct a leadership program for rural health workers. He saw the importance of teaching the leadership practices to frontline health workers who were frustrated in their attempts to provide quality services to a poor population. He was committed to improving these services. His invitation was the beginning of a long professional and personal relationship that changed our lives and the lives of many around the world.

To launch a program, we had to first align MSH's key stakeholder, the United States Agency for International Development (USAID), to fund a pilot leadership program for teams of rural health workers for one year. They chose to fund it because the program was aligned with their own mission of improving the health results for the poor in Egypt.

We led the pilot program with ten participating teams from rural health facilities in the rural governorate of Aswan, where health indicators were low. Participants in ten health facility teams learned how to apply the leadership practices to make breakthroughs in the number and quality of health services they provided for poor patients. After one year of applying the practices, their results included marked increases in the number of women using family-planning and maternity services.

Despite the success of the program, it was not funded for a second year. When we sadly announced to participants that the program would end, a local obstetrician from

Aswan, Dr. Abdo Al Swasy, said, "Don't worry! We'll do it ourselves!" His purpose, "to improve health care for poor women in Aswan," moved him to reach beyond his medical training to learn how to lead and facilitate a leadership program for health teams across the Aswan governorate. When I asked him years later what had motivated him to sustain the program, he said, "It produced the results I cared about!" We have found through the *Leading for Results* practices that when people achieve the results they care about, they are inspired to take on new challenges.

Over a three-year period, a core team of local doctors and nurses trained five "generations" of leadership facilitators (more than three dozen people). These facilitators trained 183 health facility teams (more than a thousand health workers) to apply the leadership practices to achieve measurable health service improvements. They did this using the resources in their hands: their own pencils, papers, materials, transport, and—most important of all—their own hearts and minds.

In the third year of the program, when all the health facility teams in Aswan (a state of over three million people) had participated in the program, the core team of leadership facilitators aligned around a new purpose: "reducing maternal mortality across the entire governorate." This purpose reflected their deep concern about correcting the conditions that were causing unnecessary deaths of women during labor and delivery.

LEARNING AND ADAPTING TO ACHIEVE RESULTS

After conferring with professors in a nearby medical school, and analyzing the root causes of the reasons that mothers were dying in childbirth, they aligned physicians and health workers in all of the rural villages around a set of protocols to reduce maternal deaths.

To reduce maternal mortality it is necessary to reduce the delays in getting pregnant women who are hemorrhaging to the right care. The leadership facilitators aligned all of the physicians in the rural villages to agree to immediately move women with troubled pregnancies out of their local health facilities to hospitals where there were qualified surgeons. They used taxis—there are no ambulances available in these rural villages—to move the women. And they called ahead with mobile phones to communicate their arrival so that teams of physicians trained in these types of complications would be ready to treat the women.

The result was spectacular. Over a two-year period, with no additional resources, they succeeded in reducing the maternal mortality rate from 85.0 per 100,000 live births to 35.5 per 100,000. This reduction in maternal mortality rate was much greater than in similar governorates in Egypt. Thanks to their efforts, many more women have survived childbirth and gone home to raise their families. These results have been documented in an article that Dr. Mansour, Dr. Al Swasy, and I wrote for the World Health Organization's journal, *Human Resources for Health.*

In subsequent years, the Leadership Development Program took on a life of its own. It has now been conducted with health managers and their teams in more than forty countries. The *Leading for Results* practices are also now a core part of the curriculum in schools of medicine and business in Africa and Latin America, and also at the Boston University School of

Public Health. Hundreds of local facilitators around the world are now trained to lead this program.

Applying the practice *Knowing your purpose* was key to aligning dozens of players to create, support, and scale up a program with real public health impact. Beyond those mentioned in this short version of the story are numerous people who made this happen. At a tenth anniversary celebration of the LDP at MSH, we read acknowledgments of the dozens of people in over forty countries who had been involved in making this program a success.

Reflection—Ask yourself:

- *Is there something "big" that I would like to accomplish in the world?*

- *Does this require that I align others with similar purposes to carry it out?*

- *What are their purposes and how can I align them around a common purpose?*

DISCOVERING YOUR PURPOSE

Purpose is the rudder that enables us to steer our lives.
—Dr. Ronald Heifetz, cofounder of the Center for Public Leadership at Harvard Kennedy School of Government

While the Egypt health workers' story is about purpose being clarified and manifested on a large scale, the same principles apply to all of our lives. When we are clear about our purpose, our actions are focused toward results we care about. It is this clarity of purpose that is key to effectiveness in all areas. The exercise below will help you discover your own purpose.

EXERCISE: WRITING YOUR PURPOSE STATEMENT

Purpose statement—A concise description of what you intend to contribute. It captures the essence, in as few words as possible, of what you are doing when you feel you are using your unique gifts and talents.

- Have a pad of paper and a pen or pencil on hand.

- You may find it helpful to share this with a trusted friend who can provide feedback and support.

- Sit comfortably, close your eyes, and take a few deep breaths to relax.

Think back on your life and identify a time when you felt deeply happy that your unique strengths and skills were being well used—a time when you were making a real contribution, one that would not have happened if you had not been there.

Do not take too long on this. Take the first image that comes to mind.

- When you see the moment in your mind, think about what you were doing.

- Who were you with and what were you doing?

- Describe this in a few words or phrases in writing.

Ask yourself:

- What am I passionate about doing?

- What is the unique contribution that I am making?

- Share what you have written with a friend and discuss: What were you uniquely contributing in the situation?

Fill in the blanks in this sentence:

I am here to _____ to _____.

Try a few versions and decide which one calls to you.

Examples of purpose statements:

- To teach leadership to high-performers who want to make a difference

- To bring good analysis to complex situations

- To bring understanding and compassion to women in need

- To bring laughter and joy to people around me

Try writing a statement that captures what you were doing when you felt "well-used."

- Test out a draft of a purpose statement and read it aloud.

- Ask yourself: Does it ring true? When you hear it, do you say **Yes**?

I have found that when people say *Yes!* to a purpose statement, that statement is usually right. When they hesitate or say *Yeah*, they need to do a little more work to find the exact words that resonate in their hearts.

Try writing some drafts of your purpose statement and testing them with others by speaking them out loud. It may feel embarrassing, as purpose statements are often "lofty." (I could think, "Who am

I, after all, to teach leadership?") But try it anyway, even if it feels embarrassing at first. People's purpose statements vary widely. They need not be particularly serious or grandiose. As you uncover the purpose that rings true for you, you will recognize it—and it will make you happy.

Your purpose statement is like a ship's rudder that will steer you through future life choices. Once you have clarified your purpose statement, you can go on to the other practices to begin achieving the results that are most important to you.

Practice Two:
Envisioning a Better Future

*Dreams are extremely important. You can't
do it unless you can imagine it.*
—George Lucas

- *How envisioning works*

- *The role of vision in effective action*

- *Knowing what you care about*

- *Truly shared visions*

- *Creating a picture of the future*

- *How an image can shape your actions*

- *The importance of knowing the current reality*

Now that you have identified—or begun to identify—your purpose statement, you want to envision what you will achieve when you manifest that purpose in reality.

I use the word *envision* because *vision* is often misunderstood and misused. Many good organizations have *vision statements* that boast that their organization will be the "best in the world" at what they do. These statements usually live on posters and wallet cards rather than in people's hearts and minds. When asked what their organization's vision is, people often need to refer to those posters and cards. This overuse of the word has diminished our recognition of the powerful role that a clear vision of the future can play in inspiring effective action.

Creating an image or vision of the future is different from knowing your purpose. Your purpose expresses *why* you do something; it is the reason for which you or your current project exists. *Envisioning*, in contrast, is *what* you, in your mind's eye, see yourself doing in the future when you are carrying out that purpose. To envision the future is to create a visual image of what we want to see come into existence. For example, when I see myself fulfilling my purpose—"teaching leadership to high-performers who want to make a difference"—I envision many ways that I can see this happening. Sometimes I see an image of inspired students in a large hall; sometimes I see the faces of other facilitators around the world teaching the leadership courses I have designed.

Forming a clear image of the future is an ongoing mental process. This is the heart of imagination, that uniquely human capability that we all have. It is such a precious gift and one that we need to nurture and use well. A vision of the future helps you to see what you want to create, what you want to bring into existence. This is different than problem solving, a process that seeks to drive unwanted conditions out of existence. You can solve all of your problems and still not achieve what you want in your life.

Once you have written your purpose statement and know what you are here to contribute, you can begin to envision what your life will look like when you are fully living your life in service of that purpose. Refer back to the purpose statement you wrote in the exercise in chapter one to move into this practice of envisioning the future.

How envisioning works

We continuously create images in our daily lives. When we wake up in the morning, we typically see in our minds the visual images of events we expect to happen in our day. For instance, you may see yourself eating breakfast, tending to children, traveling to work, or getting together with colleagues or friends. All these anticipated activities get started as images in your brain before you act. Once you see an image of yourself doing something you intend to do, you start to act in ways that will move you closer to doing it. This is the way your brain moves you from image to action in everyday life. Kerry Johnson, a colleague and my coauthor in adult learning, describes this when he says: "Thought is trial action."

To achieve the results we most care about, we may need to adopt new thinking and actions, and it is critical to understand what motivates us to change our thoughts and behaviors. Behaving in new ways requires that we engage in two activities: 1) We need to see a clear mental picture of a different and better future that we want—one that we can see, touch, and feel in our imagination. 2) We must actively participate in the process of analyzing the obstacles to our intended results and arriving at new actions that will move us toward that desired future.

We need to engage in these two activities because we humans don't easily change our behaviors when other people's solutions are imposed on us (or even suggested to us). But when we are involved in analyzing our situation and finding solutions ourselves, we more readily own and implement new behaviors. Effective mothers realize this when they ask young children who are reluctant to get dressed to choose whether they want to wear the green or blue pants today. The child, who is now participating in the process of assessing and choosing, is usually eager to move into action. (I learned this from my own mother, and it proved to be very helpful in early-morning rush situations.) We act most effectively when we are involved in assessing and choosing our actions.

The *Leading for Results* practices give us the ability to both envision the future and choose effective actions ourselves. This is why the practices have proven to be effective in producing results around the world, even in situations where people were previously in despair.

Images of bad outcomes can influence our actions as well. We project bad outcomes in our everyday thoughts through worries and fears about the future. For example, we might imagine that someone will think badly about our work, so we become overly anxious when presenting it. These images do not usually bring out the most productive behavior; therefore, we need to be careful about the negative images we put in our brains when we worry.

Sometimes, of course, worrisome images can be useful in propelling us to protect ourselves from real dangers. Images about getting hit by a car make us more cautious as we cross streets. At other times, however, imagined threats can paralyze us, preventing any forward motion toward our goals. Our fears can take on a reality in our minds. As Mark Twain said, "Most of my worst problems never happened!"

Fortunately, our ability to be conscious about our thoughts allows us to be aware of how our thoughts about the future can impact our attitudes and our actions. It is very important to use our ability to envision the future in ways that serve us. We don't want to put images of outcomes we don't want in our brains!

Reflection—Ask yourself:

- *What outcomes do I want to bring into existence?*

- *What pictures of the future am I putting in my brain?*

- *How can I reinforce the positive outcomes I want by imagining them more clearly?*

STORY: EMPLOYEES IMAGINING A BETTER FUTURE FOR THEIR COLLEGE

I consulted to a Boston-area college that was trying to improve their departments through a process-improvement program. When I asked department managers what their vision was—how they saw their departments in the future—they answered that the future was being decided for them by upper-level managers in charge of the improvement process; they had no say in it. The organization had communicated its change initiative in such a way as to disempower its most vital resource—the ability of its employees to imagine a better future that they could work toward! As we talked, the managers began to see that they needed all their collective wisdom to create a comprehensive vision and plan for the future.

They got back in touch with their purpose, which was to provide the best possible learning environment for their students. Then each department was able to envision how it could optimize its function in the future in a way that students would be served better.

For example, the college bookstore saw itself as serving students in a greater variety of formats, and implemented a feedback process by which they were able to hear students' points of view about the best way to supply course reading materials. It was especially important to include students' input in the design of the bookstore's process at a time when online resources were just becoming available.

The staff became engaged in designing processes to better serve the students in a rapidly changing environment. Their morale was improved as they began to play an active role in both seeing the future, and participating in analyzing and choosing actions to move toward that future.

Reflection—Ask yourself:

- *Are you in the midst of a change that you feel someone else is in charge of?*

- *What future can you envision in this change—one that inspires you and will lead to results you care about?*

- *What actions would be effective in moving toward that future?*

THE ROLE OF VISION IN EFFECTIVE ACTION

The ability to imagine the future is key to all successful endeavors, whether they are managerial, personal, or even scientific. The following story illustrates how envisioning the future can be key to scientific outcomes.

STORY: SEEING A BETTER FUTURE FOR PATIENTS AND THEIR FAMILIES

I recently worked with a team leader in a pharmaceutical company doing cancer research. He was an experienced biochemist but a relatively new team leader, and he had not yet realized the power of envisioning with his team. (He later confessed that he originally considered "vision" one more hokey idea from Human Resources.)

But after he worked with his team to create a shared vision of what they wanted their research to accomplish when their drug was successful, including a clear image of how this work would contribute to saving lives, he reported that his team members began to be more motivated. When the researchers began to actively create images of recovering patients and relieved families in their minds, they set goals that they were more passionate about meeting. As he puts it, "Now they can *see* it; they are much clearer about what we're doing and why."

Reflection—Ask yourself:

- *Is there some important activity you are involved in for which there is no future vision?*

- *What picture of the future could inspire you to take more effective actions?*

- *How can you share this image with others?*

KNOWING WHAT YOU CARE ABOUT

I often ask people what they most care about. This question puts them directly in touch with what they really want to accomplish. The story below shows how a committed group of executives imagined what they wanted to leave behind - to their company and their families.

STORY: LEAVING A LEGACY

I was fortunate to be able to talk with a group of senior managers from Korea's LG Group in the 1990s when their companies were aspiring to become global leaders. They had inherited a traditional management structure and culture that did not always encourage innovation. They wanted to break out of patterns that held them back from the type of creative thinking necessary for global growth and leadership. I met in Seoul with the presidents from six LG companies to talk about leading a learning organization. We discussed how the individual's capacity to envision the future is crucial to learning and change.

These presidents were clear about their purpose: to be global leaders in their industries. I asked them to imagine their futures when they were satisfied that they had accomplished their purpose. I also asked them what they cared about deeply and personally, and where they wanted to be in ten years. Their responses were moving. When thinking into the future, they said they wanted to be thought of as people who had led their organizations well and earned the trust of their employees. Others said that they wanted to be alive and in good health, and not a burden to their families.

The participants commented that this was the first time they had talked with each other about what they most cared about. Their traditional educational system had trained them only to receive information, not to see themselves as creators of new knowledge based on what they envisioned for the future. They began to see that envisioning the future and learning and adapting to rapid change were necessary practices for their organizations in order for them to become global leaders in their industries.

Reflection—Ask yourself:

* *What do you most care about?*

* *What do you want to bring into existence?*

* *What do you personally want to see as a result of this change?*

It is important when working in groups to create visions of the future that are truly shared and not just the vision of the person in charge. In the story below global executivees struggle to learn what a truly shared vision is.

STORY: CREATING TRULY SHARED VISIONS

I worked with a multinational manufacturing company over many years. At an offsite meeting with the firm's senior executives from around the world, when I asked what their company's vision was, the chief executive officer said, "The vision is clear—it is *my* vision!" Looking out at a roomful of executives sitting in awkward silence, I asked, "Is this true? Do you all share his vision of the future?" One relatively young and new manager had the courage to speak up and said, "Well, actually, I don't really know what his vision of the future is." This broke the silence, triggering a heated debate about what a shared vision really is. Was it just adopting the vision of the top leader, or was it engaging all levels in imaging a better future?

This meeting was remembered as a turning point for the company. Executives began to see the importance of meeting with their teams and departments to engage in the practice of including others in envisioning the future. Their willingness to be honest about this issue, and to confront each other with their genuine questions and concerns, enabled them to open up to a more inclusive process for exploring their company's vision for the future.

Envisioning the future became an ongoing organizational practice. Many valuable new strategic and operational ideas began to emerge from all levels of the organization, including from the front line of mechanics, who, when asked what they envisioned for the future, came up with innovative ideas for improving their service business.

CREATING A PICTURE OF THE FUTURE

To get a clear vision of the future it is helpful to work directly with pictures. To get out of the verbal and analytical part of your brains, it is helpful to draw a picture of what you would most like to see happen in the future. Pictures can be powerful motivators, conveying meaning directly, without the intervention of words.

The story below, from Afghanistan, is my favorite story about the power of creating a picture of the future. In this example we see how envisioning the future is such a core human capability that even decades of war and grinding poverty cannot extinguish it.

STORY: DRAWING A PICTURE OF THE FUTURE IN RURAL AFGHANISTAN

The most memorable picture in all of my years of teaching leadership came from a health facility team in rural Afghanistan. This health facility was located in Bamiyan, the province that became famous when giant Buddha statues were dynamited there in 2001.

Dr. Mansour and I traveled to rural Afghanistan to introduce the MSH Leadership Development Program there in 2005. When we asked a team of health workers from a rural facility to draw what they most dreamed of, they talked together for a while and then drew a picture of "healthy children walking to school on safe roads." I found this vision deeply moving. For these rural Afghans, all aspects of this vision were nonexistent— the health of their children, the availability of schools, *and* safe roads.

They decided to move toward their vision by increasing the number of young children who were being vaccinated against preventable childhood illnesses. They explored what obstacles they needed to overcome and what was in their control to change. They saw that they had resources in their hands to immunize the children. But among their primary obstacles was that people in the villages had to travel many miles over difficult roads to get to the health facility. More importantly, many did not believe in the benefits of immunization.

To address these obstacles the team began by sending the "vaccinator"—a big man in a traditional Afghan turban—to travel to the remote areas to educate village and religious leaders, explaining the effectiveness of immunizations, and training the local leaders to be health educators in their villages. These local leaders encouraged families to have their children immunized. By creating a vision, identifying the results they wanted to achieve, and making plans to overcome obstacles, this health team increased immunization coverage in their area from 10 percent to over 60 percent in just a few months.

How an image can shape your actions

When vision is used as a field of sight, it opens a range of new possibilities, not just in the future but also in the present. For example, when you imagine buying a new model of car, you create an image of that car in your head. Suddenly you begin to see that car model everywhere!

When I was a young professional, I created a vision of being a "master teacher." I put a painting on my wall of a teacher in front of a group of eager students under a tree with only a board to write on. To me this image illustrated what a master teacher should be able to do: use only his or her commitment and knowledge to teach students in an inspired way.

To move into this vision I worked over many years apprenticing to master teachers. I observed great teachers, such as Ronald Heifetz from Harvard, who always challenged his students to more deeply understand and manifest their purpose; Eleanor Duckworth, also from Harvard, who could lead an entire class by asking only a few questions; and Peter Senge from MIT, who always took great care to listen carefully to understand how each student thought, especially those who did not make sense at first. Being in their presence enabled me to see how I wanted to manifest my vision as a master teacher.

I designed the Leadership Development Program in this image. There are no PowerPoint slides, and no technology is needed for local program facilitators in low-resource settings to teach leadership. With only one program guide and a blackboard, or paper taped to a wall to write on, they can conduct a leadership program over a six-month period.

My vision of the simple teacher under a tree has guided my choices in all my program design work. I create programs that people can use with no extra materials or special training. This image has also guided my own teaching; to this day I am still one of very few university teachers who do not use PowerPoint slides. I am inspired by my vision to create learning environments in which I can see students who are eagerly participating in their own learning.

THE IMPORTANCE OF KNOWING THE CURRENT REALITY

Having an image of the future you want is key to achieving it. But knowing the current reality—where you are now—is also critically important; without knowing the way things really are, you will not be able to effectively move toward your vision. When you are embarking on a journey, and are mapping your route to a destination, it is critical to know where you are starting from.

Sometimes visionaries are called "dreamers," meaning people who are not in touch with reality. If you want to be taken seriously, you need to demonstrate that you understand the current reality.

STORY:TELLINGTHETRUTHABOUTTHECURRENTREALITY

I once worked with a consumer goods company that was trying to improve their customer satisfaction ratings. Their vision was for the majority of their customers to be satisfied. I asked the managers how many customers were currently satisfied. They hesitated to tell me, but finally admitted that only 10 percent were. They were afraid to reveal this information to their staff, because they didn't want them to be demoralized.

These managers failed to realize that by not telling the truth about the current situation, they risked having their staff underestimate the gap, and the work that was needed to close that gap. When you encourage people not only to dream, but also to tell the truth about the current reality, you support them analyzing what of the obstacles are and what needs to be done. Only in this way can they realistically move toward their vision of the future.

EXERCISE: ENVISIONING A BETTER FUTURE

If one advances confidently in the direction of his dreams, and endeavors to live the life which he has imagined, he will meet with success unexpected in common hours.
—Henry David Thoreau

Have on hand a large piece of unlined drawing paper and colored markers or crayons.

Sit in a quiet place. Put your feet flat on the floor, and feel grounded in your chair. Take a few slow, deep breaths and relax.

First look at your purpose statement. Reflect on what that means to you and why this purpose enables you to contribute in the ways that are most important to you.

Then take a few minutes to see a picture of your life a year or two from now when you are fulfilling this purpose.

Imagine the following, without putting limitations on any of these images for now:

- See your health in an ideal state.

- What do you see yourself doing to maintain this good health?

- See yourself in one important relationship.

- What do you see yourself doing in that relationship when it is exactly the way you want it to be?

- See the work you are contributing to the world.

- What are you doing and whom are you serving when you are doing the work that is most important to you?

Once you have seen an image for each of these areas of your life, jot down a few notes, or draw images of the answers as they appeared to you.

Then share your vision with another person.

Share the images in the present tense as if they were already happening, for example:

- I am thin and fit and go to the gym every day.

- I am in loving regular contact with my grown children.

- I am serving others by teaching them what I know about producing results.

To reinforce your vision, share this again with another person.

- Feel free to adapt and add more elements as you get more comfortable speaking your vision out loud.

Stating these visions in the present tense brings them into the "field" of existence.

When you speak them to others, they begin to become part of the reality you experience. What you speak is very powerful. Your actions will begin to match what you see yourself doing.

EXERCISE: CREATING A VISION BOARD TO REINFORCE YOUR PERSONAL VISION

Take a pile of old magazines and tear out any images that are appealing to you. Don't do a lot of thinking about this! Go with your gut impulses. Choose whatever images call to you; later you can reflect on what in the images spoke to you, and which images you want to incorporate into your vision. You might be surprised by what attracts you.

Trim the images with scissors if you like, or leave them with torn edges if you prefer them that way. Arrange them on a poster board, moving them around until their pattern pleases you, and then attach the pictures to the board using a glue stick, paste, or tape. Once you have assembled the images, study the overall collage. Which aspects of it are calling to you most strongly? Which ones do you want to incorporate into your life?

Show it to others and explain it to them. Place it where you will see it regularly—near your breakfast table, on your mirror, or beside your desk—and look at it every day.

Some years ago I created two vision boards, one for where I wanted to live—someplace with large trees in the backyard and close to the center of Boston; and another for the work I wanted to do—teaching leadership at prestigious universities and writing books that leave a legacy. These pictures guide my actions and decisions every day and have shaped several specific results. My current home looks out on many large trees, and I live within easy driving distance of Boston clients. I teach at Boston University, and I write and publish the leadership lessons I have learned and want to share.

I have a right to dream!
—Dr. Mohamed Souror[1]

EXERCISE: CREATING SHARED VISION IN A GROUP

This exercise guides a group through the process of creating a shared vision, using images and pictures rather than words.

- *If the group is large, ask them to work in smaller groups of three to six people.*

- *For each group, have a large piece of paper and colored markers or crayons for all participants.*

First, make sure people understand the purpose or mission of their organization or group—what are they here to do; what is their primary purpose?

---

1   Health manager in Aswan, Egypt, and facilitator of the LDP, responding to his superiors when they told him the family-planning targets he chose were too high and that he was a "dreamer."

Then ask everyone to dream about the future of their group or organization.

What do they see happening when they are manifesting their purpose well?

- Who are they serving?

- What does that look like when they are doing it well?

- How are they working together?

- What is the quality of their work?

To be truly creative:

- Don't concern yourself now with the obstacles to achieving that future (you will get to obstacles later in this process!).

- Don't think about not having enough time or enough money.

Let yourself go:

- Don't worry about any lack of artistic ability!

- Just draw what you would most like to see happen.

- Have each person make a quick sketch and share their drawings with others before creating the larger picture.

Prepare one shared drawing.

- Have the small group prepare one large (flipchart-size) drawing that captures the collective dreams of the members of the group.

- All should participate in this drawing. You don't need artistic ability—stick figures will do!

Present the drawings to the larger group.

- Invite each small group to present its large drawing to others present.

- Ask if someone who can write well will transform the elements of the vision into words.

Remember: it is the process of envisioning together, not the end product, that is key. The written vision statement is only the "memory" of the experience of seeing a future together!

Although people love seeing the drawings and hearing about them, presenting written vision statements is oftentimes not inspiring to others who weren't involved in the envisioning process. What is inspiring is asking others what they see in the future, and including their thoughts in an expanded, shared vision.

Too many senior management groups make the mistake of writing the vision and then thinking that sharing that written statement with their colleagues is leadership. People want to be included in the vision and asked what *they* see, what *their* image of the future is. Only by inquiring in this way can we truly tap into people's creative energies to create the future together.

Practice Three:
Clarifying Your Challenge

Sometimes all you need to lead is a good question.
—Ronald Heifetz

- *Framing your challenge*

- *Defining a specific and measurable result*

- *Working in your sphere of influence*

- *Staying realistic and time-bound*

- *Assessing the current situation*

- *Identifying obstacles and analyzing root causes*

- *Using the Results Model*

Once you have identified your purpose and created a vision of the future you want, the next step is to clarify your challenge in a way that inspires you and others to overcome obstacles and achieve results. The act of clarifying or *framing* your challenge guides your thinking and actions as you begin to manifest your purpose. It also provides the framework to involve others in your challenge.

FRAMING YOUR CHALLENGE

When you *frame your challenge*, you clarify both the results you want and the obstacles you need to overcome to accomplish that result. Your challenge is framed as a question: *"How will I accomplish the results I want in the light of the obstacles I am facing?"* Framing the challenge as a question recognizes that there are often no easy answers to complex challenges, and that others need to become involved in finding solutions. The challenge, properly framed, becomes the leadership question you will use to engage others around your intended result.

The challenge question contains two major elements: 1) the result you want, and 2) the obstacles you need to overcome to achieve that result. You write it in this format: *"How can we achieve X result in the light of Y obstacles?"* For example, "How can we increase the number of services our company is offering when we are being pressed for cost-cutting measures?" Or, as in the Afghan health worker's story, "How can we increase the number of children being immunized when people do not trust the health facilities?"

In framing your challenge, it's important to remember that *challenge* is not merely a more optimistic way to say *problem*. A challenge contains in it both a result you want, and an obstacle to be overcome. Problems are conditions that are in the way of achieving results we want. The problem is not a challenge all in itself.

For example *poverty* is a terrible condition, but it is not a challenge unless there is a result we want to accomplish. "How do we improve the health of our citizens in light of poverty?" is a challenge that a health system might take on as its own. A challenge is something we choose to own and take on because we are committed to the result. A problem is usually something we see as occurring outside of ourselves.

This distinction between a challenge and a problem is an important one. Often in workshops in poor countries, people are asked to list all the problems they are confronting in their work. After they have finished making the long list of problems, they generally feel pretty demoralized. In contrast, discussions of challenges can be inspiring, because each challenge includes a reference to a result they care about, one that will lead them closer to their vision of the future.

A well-framed challenge helps us maintain an energizing focus on that result. As Tomé Ca, a health information systems officer in the West Africa Health Organization who took part in an MSH Leadership Development Program, said, "A challenge motivates me to take responsibility for my ideas and to take action on them."

I often ask people in the poorer countries to think of challenges they have faced in their personal lives—results that they wanted to achieve in the face of obstacles they needed to overcome. Doctors, for instance, frequently tell me that they were committed to finishing medical school, but that financial problems in their families, or sometimes even the death of a parent, became enormous obstacles. The challenge they took on was "How to finish medical school in the face of shrinking family resources?" When they tell their stories about how they faced this challenge, you can see the deep pride they feel in having earned their medical degrees in spite of the obstacles. This inquiry also shows people that they are already successful at facing challenges and achieving results.

Reflection—Ask yourself:

When you reflect on the challenges you have encountered in your own life

- *What are you most proud of?*

- *What strengths did it take to face this challenge? (For most of us, facing major challenges takes qualities such as persistence and commitment.)*

- *What are the lessons you have learned in facing challenges in your life?*

To lead effectively, you will need to get clear about the results you are committed to, and the challenges you will need to face. Then you will use your strengths to overcome the obstacles in your path.

DEFINING A SPECIFIC AND MEASURABLE RESULT

The first result you choose will represent just one element of your vision. You will take one aspect of your vision and begin to make progress toward it. If you can achieve that result, you will move closer to realizing your entire vision. And you will learn how to accomplish other results you care about.

To ensure that your first desired result is clearly defined, describe it specifically enough so that an outsider could assess whether you had accomplished it or not. Toward that end, your result needs to be specific and measurable. For example, rather than say your result is "I want to be in good health," to be specific you can say, "In the next six months my weight will be reduced by 10 percent and I will have a plan in place to maintain that weight loss."

I have found that almost everyone, regardless of their level of education, has great difficulty clearly stating their results. This makes sense: after all, when a result is specific and measurable, with a clear time period in which to achieve it, we can be held accountable for either succeeding or failing to produce it!

Saying we will be accountable to produce a specific result commits us to thinking in new ways and taking on new actions—sometimes outside of the things we are used to doing. When the Afghan health workers committed to immunizing more children, they had to go outside of the walls of their clinic and begin to interact with people in the community in a new way. This was necessary to achieve the result of increasing the number of children being immunized.

WORKING IN YOUR SPHERE OF INFLUENCE

In addition to being specific and measurable, your desired first result also needs to be appropriate to your own sphere of influence, or to that of your team. For example, the Afghan health team's vision was "healthy children walking to school on safe roads." If this health facility team had chosen as its measurable result "building roads in our area," that result would likely have been outside their sphere of influence. Working on results that contributed to improved children's health was within their sphere of influence and something they could begin to work on with the resources they had.

I teach this useful distinction around the world because it saves people from the frustration of wasting their efforts trying to change things that they cannot change. To choose the right measurable result, you need to understand your sphere of influence—the things that are under your control and influence to change. It is helpful to analyze in which of three spheres of activity the result is located:

- *The activities over which you have direct control*

- *The activities that you can influence*

- *The activities over which you have no influence or control*

Stephen Covey distinguished these three spheres in his book *The Seven Habits of Highly Effective People*:

Sphere of control
> We have control over most of our own behaviors, attitudes, and actions. (But this is not always easy or apparent!)

Sphere of influence
> We can influence the actions and thoughts of our families, friends, colleagues, and work environments.

Outside of our control or influence
> We cannot normally control or influence the weather, national government policies, the actions of other organizations that fall far outside our personal reach, or the thoughts and behaviors of people with whom we have no contact.

The irony is that oftentimes people's conversations are about those things in the third sphere—the things they cannot affect. Though it can be amusing to talk about the activities of others outside of our influence, it can also be an enormous waste of time.

Reflection—Ask yourself:

- *Where do I spend most of my energies—in which sphere?*

- *What sphere is the source of many of my worries and conversations?*

- *What result can I choose in an area over which I have control or influence?*

Your measurable result should be something either in your sphere of control or under your influence. When we focus our thoughts and energies on things that are out of our control and influence, we waste precious time and resources.

STAYING REALISTIC AND TIME-BOUND

> *Think big. Start small. Act now!*
> —Barnabas Suebu, Governor of Papua

Your measurable result also needs to be realistic. It should be enough of a stretch that you can use your *Leading for Results* practices in pursuing it, but not so difficult that you will never attain it within the time and resources available to you.

Your result also needs to be defined in time. You need to state by when you will accomplish it. From one to six months is generally a good length of time to focus on a result. That is long enough to accomplish something significant, but short enough not to forget what you are doing.

SMART RESULTS

A good way to remember what makes up a well-defined result is the well-known acronym *SMART*:

*S*pecific—so that you and others know exactly what you are working toward

*M*easurable—to allow you to evaluate the extent to which you achieve it

*A*ppropriate—within your sphere of influence

*R*ealistic—achievable within the time and resources available

*T*ime-bound—having a defined period for completion

In considering the SMART criteria for your intended result, think about whether the obstacles that you will need to address are sufficiently under your control or influence to allow you to affect change. Keep in mind that you may need to adjust the result after assessing the current situation and identifying your obstacles.

STORY: FOCUSING ON RESULTS IN RURAL TANZANIA

A story from leadership development work in rural Tanzania illustrates the process of successfully framing a challenge.

In 2005 I was working with health workers in the rural province of Kigoma in western Tanzania on the shores of Lake Tanganyika. In this poor province women gave birth to an average of six children each, and health services for family-planning were not easily accessible or well utilized.

I had been asked to bring the MSH Leadership Development Program to Kigoma for health managers and their teams to help increase the number of new family-planning users. EngenderHealth, a global organization committed to supporting family-planning around the world, together with Tanzania's Ministry of Health and Social Welfare (MOHSW) sponsored the program.

Flying to Kigoma from the capital, Dar es Salaam, took three hours in a plane ride that felt like being in a dented tin can. The experience of the flight brought home to me just how far into the heart of Africa we were traveling. Although many of the district managers in Kigoma spoke English, I quickly discovered that most of the participating health workers spoke only Swahili.

To enable everyone's full participation in the program, my colleague and friend Mary Mujomba from Kenya and I led the program together. Mary, who speaks Swahili, first watched me facilitate and then took over the leadership of the sessions, translating my remarks into Swahili on the spot. This was a true just-in-time transfer of capabilities!

The participating health teams worked to identify the mission of the MOHSW, the organization that they worked for. It took several hours of discussion and debate and help from their senior managers to clarify that mission. This happens in many organizations that I work with. Most people are not clear about the purpose of the organizations they work for.

The mission of the Tanzania's MOHSW was "Prevent the spread of infectious disease, and promote the health of women, children, and men." This preventive mission of the Ministry of Health is often not well-communicated to frontline workers at the health facilities, who are faced daily with long lines of people seeking urgent curative medical care.

Once they clarified this mission, the health workers created a vision of a future when they were implementing the preventative part of their work. They did this in their teams by drawing colored pictures of the future they wanted. In their images they drew communities with healthy children where all women had access to family-planning.

When they saw this vision of the future, they began to identify measurable results that were within their control and influence. Together, the health facility teams chose "increasing the number of new clients

> for family-planning." They set a desired measurable result of increasing the average number of new family-planning clients in the nine health sites by 20 percent in one year.

ASSESSING THE CURRENT SITUATION

Once you have defined a specific, measurable result, you are ready to look at the current conditions in your environment in relation to that result. Being aware of the obstacles you are facing will help you choose activities to move toward your intended result.

The most important thing about assessing the current situation is to tell the truth! Don't underestimate or overestimate your current situation. Just take stock of where you are now in relation to the result you want. If possible, this current reality should also be expressed in measurable terms.

> ### STORY (CONT.): FACING THE CURRENT SITUATION
>
> For example, in Tanzania the teams wanted to increase the number of women using family-planning services, but first they had to find out their current situation. After going back to their work sites to study their data, they were dismayed to discover that many health facilities were seeing fewer than ten women a month for family-planning. This made the gap between the present condition and the desired result that much greater and inspired them to work that much harder.

IDENTIFYING OBSTACLES AND ANALYZING ROOT CAUSES

Once you have identified the obstacles in your path, you need to determine their underlying causes in order to know how to address them. This process is called root cause analysis. By examining the root causes of the obstacles, you will not only understand the obstacles better but also be able to choose actions that address the underlying problem, not just the symptoms that you can easily see. If we only treat the symptoms, we will not eliminate the cause of those symptoms. For example, if you only treat the heat of a fever, you may fail to identify the underlying infection that is causing it.

STORY (CONT.): UNDERSTANDING THE ROOT CAUSES

In Kigoma, Tanzania, the symptom was that women were not coming to the health facilities to use family-planning services.

The teams worked together to understand the root cause of this lack of attendance at the clinic. They asked:

- *Did the women not trust the competency of the health workers?*

- *Why were they mistrustful of the services?*

- *Why did they not understand the importance of family-planning to women's health?*

ASKING "WHY?"

When you identify an obstacle in the way of achieving your result, ask, "Why is that true?" or "Why is that happening?" To each answer, ask *Why?* again. Continue asking *Why?* until the answer is something on which you can take action. This is a technique derived from the Japanese quality-improvement movement that encourages you to ask *Why?* until you get to the root of an issue.

STORY(CONT.):FRAMINGTHECHALLENGEANDACHIEVING RESULTS

The teams in Tanzania analyzed the root causes of the obstacles so they could focus their efforts on the activities that were most critical to overcoming each obstacle. Through this process they realized that people were not using the family-planning services currently available because of a few key obstacles, including low community awareness about the health benefits of family-planning and a shortage of staff skilled in family-planning.

They framed their leadership challenge as follows: *"How can we increase the number of family-planning clients in light of low community awareness of the importance of family-planning for maternal and child health and not enough adequately trained personnel?"*

They prioritized actions that they could take by using their own resources and also aligning the resources of key stakeholders. They increased on-the-job training of health workers in family-planning and made alliances with village leaders to raise awareness of the importance of family-planning for maternal and child heath.

In assessing their own available resources, they realized that they had a mobile van that they were not using. So they dedicated this van to providing outreach services in family-planning. As of December 2006, one year after the start of the LDP, the average number of *new* family-planning clients per month had increased from twenty-seven per month at the health centers and district hospital to forty per month.

Heartened by the success of their first effort at achieving a significant result, the teams were inspired to take on other challenges, including the renovation of a health facility. At the International Conference on Family Planning in Uganda in 2011, Juliana Bantambya, the nurse-manager and leader of this effort for EngenderHealth, proudly showed the family-planning results and photos of the renovated facility. I was privileged to share the presentation with her.

THE RESULTS MODEL

At the end of this chapter is a picture of a model you can use to frame your challenge called the Results Model. This diagram provides a systematic method that will help you think through the process of facing your challenge.

It represents the organizational learning work of Peter Senge, which uses "creative tension" to show the gap between the result you want and your current situation. It frames the challenge as a question for you to share with others—a leadership lesson that I learned from Ronald Heifetz. The model uses tools from the quality-improvement methodology to analyze the obstacles and choose priority actions.

During my work at Management Sciences for Health (MSH),[2] I learned the importance of identifying short-term measurable results that can move you closer to your vision of the future. Working with leadership teams around the world we synthesized a Challenge Model that enables teams to work towards a shared vision together. This model is now used around the world in the MSH Leadership Development Programs.

---

2   Bragar Mansour, et al., *Managers Who Lead: A Handbook for Improving Health Services*, (Cambridge, MA: Management Sciences for Health, 2005).

The Results Model builds on that work. The Results Model is not a problem-solving process. It is a *leading for results* process that frames the challenge you and others will face. It helps individuals and teams bring new things into existence that they care about.

In the exercises at the end of first two chapters you have addressed two questions you need to answer to begin filling this model out. First, you need to first be clear about your purpose statement—what are you here to do. Then, you need to have a vision about what you imagine will happen in the future when you are succeeding at that purpose.

In the Results Model you will fill in your purpose and your vision, and then you will include one measurable result that will move you closer to that purpose and vision.

To identify a measurable result, pick one aspect of your vision that you want to work on. Identify one result that will move you closer to realizing that aspect of your vision. Remember that your desired result needs to be SMART: specific, measurable, appropriate, realistic, and time-bound.

After you have identified your result and the current situation in relationship to that result, you then identify the obstacles in the way to that result. You look deeply to understand the root cause of those obstacles.

Now you can frame your challenge as a question:

- *How can we achieve _____ (measurable result) in the light of _____ (obstacles we need to overcome)?*

Once this challenge is framed as a question, you can start to identify the actions needed to (1) address the root causes of the obstacles, and (2) move you closer to your desired result. You can also use this question to share your challenge with others.

The steps for filling out the Results Model are in the exercise below:

EXERCISE: USING THE RESULTS MODEL

Step 1. Review your purpose statement.

Write your purpose at the top of the model.

Step 2. Envision the future, when you are accomplishing your purpose.

Write a few words about what want to see in the future.

Put these in the Vision cloud.

Step 3. Choose a measurable result.

Pick an aspect of your vision, and create one specific measurable result that will move you closer to that vision.

This result should be achievable in one to six months.

Step 4. Assess the current situation.

What conditions describe the current situation in relation to your intended result? Write a few of these at the bottom of the model.

Include both enabling and difficult conditions.

You now have the gap between your intended result and the current situation.

Step 5. Identify the obstacles and their root causes.

Make a list of obstacles that you will have to overcome to move from your current situation to your intended result.

Ask *Why?* several times to analyze the underlying causes of these obstacles to make sure you are addressing the root causes and not just the symptoms.

Step 6. Clarify your challenge and select priority actions.

Ask: "How will I achieve _____ (my measurable result) in the light of _____ (the root cause obstacles)?"

Write this challenge question at the bottom of the model.

Step 7. Develop and implement an action plan.

Select priority actions that you will implement to address the root causes and move you toward your result.

Make a plan for each action, including resources needed and dates due.

Step 8. Monitor your progress toward results.

Choose measures that will help you track your progress.

Once you have your challenge framed, you can use the Results Model to align your stakeholders around the results you all want. This is how you begin to engage others to lead for results. Practice Four: Aligning Your Stakeholders shows you how to do this.

THE RESULTS MODEL

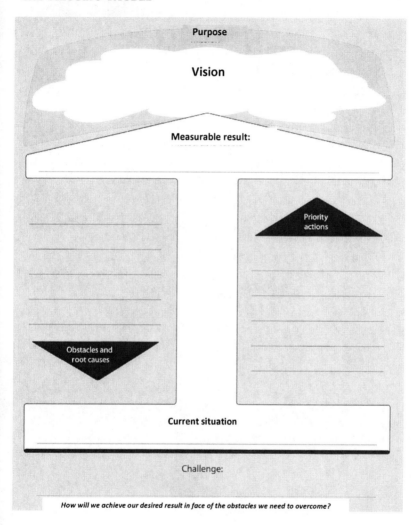

Practice Four:
Aligning Your Stakeholders

Never judge a man until you have walked a mile in his moccasins.
—Cherokee saying

- *Identify your stakeholders*

- *Know your stakeholders' interests*

- *Mobilize your stakeholders*

- *Build trust with your stakeholders*

- *Acknowledge stakeholders for their contributions*

IDENTIFY YOUR STAKEHOLDERS

For almost all the important achievements in our lives, we need the involvement of others, whether as active participants or providers of financial or emotional support. So once you have framed your challenge, it becomes critically important to identify the people you need to involve. These are your *stakeholders*.

Stakeholders are people who have something at stake in the

result you are trying to accomplish. They perceive that the accomplishment of that result either is or is not in their interest. It is important for you to understand their perceptions because they can either help you or hinder you. You need to understand both the people you need to support you in achieving the result you desire, and those who can prevent you from achieving that result. To lead effectively you will need to know what these stakeholders are interested in, and what they are most concerned about. In short, you need to put yourself in their shoes.

Stakeholders frequently have resources that you need, including material resources, knowledge, or decision-making power. Oftentimes resources that exist in an organization or a community go untapped or underused because people who could use them are not skilled at aligning their stakeholders. For example, in the Afghanistan example, the community leaders were important stakeholders with the power to help or hinder the activities of the health facility. But the health workers needed to learn how to align them to use their personal influence with families to advocate for the use of immunizations.

After using the Results Model to identify the obstacles that could prevent you from achieving your result, you can begin to talk to key stakeholders to gain their perspectives on how to overcome the obstacles.

Reflection—Ask yourself:

- *Who are the stakeholders that need to be involved in accomplishing this result?*

- *Who could help? Who could hinder?*

- *What resources do they have that could support this result?*

KNOW YOUR STAKEHOLDERS' INTERESTS

To align stakeholders effectively, you need to identify their interests and know how to best get their support. For example, in the following story from Afghanistan, committed health workers were able to save many mothers' lives because they learned how to align the stakeholders who had resources they needed.

STORY: ALIGNING STAKEHOLDERS TO PROMOTE SAFE CHILDBIRTH IN AFGHANISTAN

In 2005, Dr. Mansour and I led a study tour of fifteen Afghan health managers to visit the Leadership Development Program that had been running on its own for more than three years in Aswan Governorate in Egypt. The visiting Afghans wanted to learn from health teams in rural Egypt how they could implement the leadership practices with health teams in their own rural provinces in Afghanistan.

The Afghans saw the commitment of health workers in Aswan to using their own resources and building good relations with stakeholders, including community and religious leaders. One of the study tour participants, a young doctor, Dr. Ihsan Ullah Shahir, who was working in Bamiyan Province in central Afghanistan, got exciting news during the study tour: he had been appointed Provincial Health Director for Bamiyan. Later that year we traveled to Bamiyan to conduct the first Afghan LDP workshop with health teams there. We traveled over nine hours on roads with potholes the size of craters and led a workshop in a room without electricity. Despite the obstacles, it was one of the most moving experiences of our lives. Because the workshop needed

---

to be conducted in the local language, Dari, we worked with an Afghan facilitator, our colleague Dr. Abdul Ali, who would translate as he learned how to lead the program himself. The MSH health project there was later able to bring the LDP to many other provinces in Afghanistan, eventually reaching thousands of Afghan health workers.

The young provincial health director, Dr. Shahir, demonstrated that he had become a master in aligning stakeholders when he took on the challenge of reducing maternal mortality in Bamiyan. He knew that access to a health facility with skilled medical staff is the number-one intervention that prevents death during childbirth. Unfortunately, women in this area had to travel many miles, often on donkeys, to reach the health facility. Often it took many hours and when they arrived it was too late to save their lives. It is estimated that 98 percent of deliveries in Bamiyan take place at home, with over 320 maternal deaths occurring each year.

Dr. Shahir aligned the local village stakeholders to build a maternity waiting home near the health facility. A maternity waiting home is a place where women can come when they are close to their due dates, so that they can access a health facility during childbirth. Dr. Shahir raised over ten thousand dollars from local people to buy the land for the building of the maternity waiting home, and enrolled an international donor to fund the construction.

"Very few women give birth in a clinic or a hospital. That's why this maternity waiting home is designed to be a place that feels like home," explained Dr. Shahir. To promote use of the new maternity waiting home, Dr. Shahir and his staff aligned community stakeholders by conducting awareness-raising sessions in area health centers, schools, and mosques.

They learned how to align the support of local religious leaders. A UNICEF report of July 2010 quotes the religious leader Baba Mohseny, speaking on behalf of religious leaders in Bamiyan: "Mullahs in this province fully support the project," he said. "To save a mother means to save a family, which is equivalent to saving the whole world."

In July 2011, health facility teams from Bamiyan and other provinces traveled to Kabul to present their results to senior officials from the Ministry of Public Health, as well as to representatives from donor organizations and United Nations' agencies. Reflecting on his experience, Dr. Shahir says, "The LDP changed my life. When I took responsibility as Bamiyan's provincial health director, I wanted to learn how to create change in my team, and myself, but I didn't have enough knowledge to do this. After the LDP training, however, I was able to put my leadership into practice very easily. I learned how to inspire and commit my staff."

The donor from USAID commented on the Afghan teams' ability to lead their stakeholders to mobilize resources:

> The results of their management and leadership shows that resources can be mobilized locally, whether these are financial, material, goodwill, political will, or extra hands to do the work that is required. Through a process of learning by doing, on the job, over time and in teams, facility staff from doctors to vaccinators and community health workers learned why a

> mission is important, how to create a shared
> vision, how to agree on a short-term measurable
> result and then do the necessary work of analyzing,
> aligning, mobilizing and inspiring to improve
> a critical preventive health service such as TB
> detection, immunization, family-planning, ante-
> natal and post-natal care and assisted deliveries.[3]
>
> Dr. Shahir, a young and committed doctor, demonstrated
> mastery of the *Aligning your Stakeholders* leadership
> practice to make major changes in the lives of poor
> women in a remote province in Afghanistan.

MOBILIZE YOUR STAKEHOLDERS

To mobilize is to move a group of people in a unified direction.
It is important to both align and mobilize your stakeholders. The
first task needed to mobilize your stakeholders to take actions that
support your results is to know them and what they care about.
People have a basic need to feel important, to feel valued, and to
feel that they are making a contribution. To work effectively with
stakeholders, you must understand their needs and concerns.

Reflection—Ask yourself:

- *What are my stakeholders interested in?*

- *What would make their jobs easier or help them to accomplish
  their own goals?*

- *What are their worries and concerns and how can I address them?*

---

3   "Afghans Health Teams Manage and Lead Better to Improve Services",
USAID Press Release Lisa Childs, Kabul, Afghanistan, July 24, 2011

STORY: MOBILIZING POLITICIANS IN KENYA

A health facility team in Kenya determined that it needed an ambulance in which to safely bring patients from remote areas. They analyzed their stakeholders' needs. One group of key stakeholders was local politicians. By listening to them carefully, they learned that what the politicians needed was publicity that links them with good deeds for the community. So the health facility team agreed that if an ambulance were purchased, there would be a big ceremony to launch it, at which the politicians would be acknowledged for their role in purchasing the ambulance. The politicians agreed—the ambulance was purchased, and a "ribbon-cutting ceremony" was held that was reported in the newspapers, much to the satisfaction of the politicians!

BUILD TRUST WITH YOUR STAKEHOLDERS

A key component in winning the active support of your stakeholders is ensuring that they trust you. They must willingly rely on your integrity, ability, and character. Of course, trust takes time to build and maintain.

Reflection—Ask yourself:

- *Think of someone you trust. What has he or she done to earn your trust?*

- *What can I learn from that person about building trust?*

- *What can I do more of to build trust with others?*

I conducted a large study of managers who were effective at

influencing and building trust among colleagues over whom they had no direct authority.[4]

The study found that people are trusted when they

- demonstrate credibility through competence and integrity;

- remain open to others' influence in making decisions; and

- are humble and can admit mistakes and doubts.

Having integrity means taking your promises seriously and doing your best to keep them. But it also means that whenever you cannot keep your commitment, you communicate quickly and clearly, and promise a new deadline for delivering what you promised. Only in this way can you and others trust your promises.

Never assume you have all of the answers. Always try to listen to those who disagree with you to understand the logic of their views. Practice saying a door-opening phrase, "you could be right." Being humble and not insisting on your viewpoint is key to building trust. Saying "I don't know" or "you could be right" are ways to demonstrate that you are open to other points of view and are willing to entertain them. Similarly, admitting your mistakes and uncertainties, while staying true to your commitments, ensures that others will trust that you are serious about learning and about finding the best way forward.

ACKNOWLEDGE STAKEHOLDERS FOR THEIR CONTRIBUTIONS

To keep your stakeholders inspired and motivated, a key leadership action is to thank others and celebrate their contributions and

---

4   Bragar, *Building and Maintaining Influence: A Study of Managers* (Forum Corporation, 1991).

accomplishments. The importance of acknowledging individuals' and teams' contributions to progress cannot be overstated. Authentically recognizing others for positive contributions is a powerful motivator. This is not to be confused with flattery, which is pandering to someone's ego. Authentic acknowledgment is recognition of the real contributions that another is making.

A recent study[5] confirmed that the single most important motivation for individuals in work situations is not salaries, bonuses, promotions, or other financial or status-related rewards, but the sensation of having made progress toward a desired goal. Yet most managers do not even recognize this form of motivation as significant!

Reflection—Ask yourself:

Have I:

- *Acknowledged others for the challenges they are facing and the progress they've made?*

- *Thanked others for their commitment and their daily efforts?*

- *Told others how their work has made a difference?*

You can acknowledge other people's efforts by thanking them directly, writing personal notes, and emphasizing their contributions in a formal work review. Better yet, acknowledge them *publicly,* in the presence of their colleagues and other stakeholders. By doing so, you will be strengthening their motivation to achieve results.

---

5   Teresa M. Amabile and Steven J. Kramer, *The Progress Principle: Using Small Wins to Ignite Joy, Engagement, and Creativity at Work* (Harvard Business Press Books, 2011).

STORY: STAKEHOLDER ALIGNMENT PROCESS AT A NASA LABORATORY

My son, Michael Meacham, is a mechanical engineer and team leader at NASA's Jet Propulsion Laboratory in California, where they built Curiosity, the Mars Science Laboratory robotic rover, which landed on Mars in August 2012. This project, which took more than ten years of design and fabrication, had an enormous number of interlocking designs that needed to be developed and delivered on a schedule that would get the rover to a predetermined launch date, set years in advance.

When I asked my son how they accomplished this, he told me that that stakeholder alignment is the number-one job of managers. He explained that there is a written communications protocol that guides stakeholder buy-in. Every design has a list of stakeholders who must sign off on it before it is declared complete. The list also stipulates which stakeholders can stop the design, and which are only consulting to it.

Each manager has dates by which the relevant stakeholders must sign off that they understand and approve the process. To ensure that the stakeholders are willing and able to do that, the manager must engage in the communication, education, and exchange that give the stakeholders the information they need in order to trust the process to sign off on the predetermined schedule. Only by professionalizing a stakeholder alignment process could NASA succeed at producing such immense, complex, and interdependent projects.

> **NASA also routinely holds acknowledgment ceremonies and awards those who have contributed significant innovations to the space program. I am proud to say my son Mike is a recipient of many of these innovation awards.**

Leading for results takes time. If you are focused and consistent, you will make steady progress toward your purpose and your vision of the future. At some point you may need to let go and accept that others may begin to play larger roles in realizing your purpose. You may move along making small changes, and then one day a major stakeholder who was not fully committed aligns with you, and you find your purpose manifested in ways that are beyond your wildest dreams!

I found this to be true in my own work with the MSH Leadership Development Program. Today the LDP that I designed with MSH has been offered in more than forty countries, delivered by hundreds of local facilitators without my direct involvement. This exponential expansion of our original LDP in Egypt happened after years of aligning stakeholders—and a great deal of letting go.

You will be successful when you accomplish the results you have envisioned. But more importantly, you will be fulfilled when you see others around you making their own commitments to achieving those results and extending that work far beyond your reach. By aligning stakeholders to face challenges and achieve results, you are turning your shared dreams for a better future into reality!

EXERCISE: ALIGNING YOUR STAKEHOLDERS

This exercise helps you identify your key stakeholders, understand their interests and concerns, and make a plan to mobilize their support.

STAKEHOLDER ANALYSIS WORKSHEET

Stakeholder group or individual	What are they most interested in? (What do they want?)	What is their biggest concern? (What are they worried about?)	What do we need to do to get their support?

In the grid, list your stakeholders—the individuals or groups who have stakes in the success of your results—in the left-hand column.

For each stakeholder, answer these questions:

- What are they most interested in?

- What do they want?

- What is their primary concern or worry?

- What do you need from them: resources, approvals, ideas, support?

- What is the specific request that you will make of them?

Use this information to understand the actions you need to take to align them to move toward your results.

EXERCISE: ACKNOWLEDGING OTHERS

This simple exercise is a surprisingly powerful way to strengthen people's commitment. Use it at meetings or events to celebrate people's efforts, progress, and results.

Give each member of a group a piece of paper and ask him or her to write one sentence for each member of the team, beginning with the phrase *"I acknowledge you for _____."*

- They can acknowledge others for whatever contributions they have made—either in results or in the quality of relationships.

- These acknowledgments can recognize things that each member has contributed to the writer of the acknowledgment or to others.

- Then have each person read his or her acknowledgments aloud to the others.

Through this process, your group members will grow more appreciative of each other's efforts and capabilities. They will deepen their commitments to producing shared results.

EXERCISE: BUILDING TRUST

Reflect on the following questions:

- Think of someone you trust. What has this person done to earn your trust?

- Think of someone you don't trust. What has this person done to lose your trust?

- What specific action can you take to improve your own trustworthiness?

What actions can you take to:

- Cooperate rather than compete?

- Support and help others?

- Admit your own mistakes and uncertainties?

What can you take away from this exercise that can help you become more trustworthy?

The first step toward building trust may be to admit that there is some absence of it!

Practice Five:
Learning and Adapting to Change

*The drive to learn starts earlier in the human being
than the sex drive, and usually lasts longer.*
—Peter Senge

- *Listen to learn*

- *Take time to reflect*

- *Lead through breakdowns*

- *Examine your assumptions*

Paul Lawrence, the late Harvard professor and a founder of the field of organizational behavior, said that human beings have four basic drives: "to acquire, defend, bond, and comprehend." When one or more of the four goes unfulfilled, we see imbalances that threaten sustained progress.

Comprehending our environment and the challenges we face is critically important to both individuals and organizations, especially in times of change. For people who want to make a difference, learning plays an essential role in our ability to adapt plans and processes to fit changing needs.

Adaptation is a key practice for leadership. In Nicaragua, in the midst of a major health-reform process, the director of the MSH Health project there observed "We put in the new health systems, but there was no one to lead them." He realized that processes are effective only when they are continually adapted to new conditions, and this continuous adaptation requires people who can lead.

Global executives who excel at working around the world have a primary competency that outshines their skills in areas such as strategy or marketing: their ability to learn in new situations. The two stories below illustrate how learning is key for organizational success.

STORY: BELIEVING THAT PEOPLE CAN LEARN

In 1995 I had the privilege of meeting Hun Jo Lee, who was then Chairman of LG Group, the Korean chaebol (conglomerate) that employed more than 160,000 people and was beginning to work globally. Dr. Lee had traveled to America to meet with consultants at Arthur D. Little, Inc., where I was working, to explore the field of organizational learning. He knew that his employees needed to learn about and adapt to a changing world in order to survive and thrive in the global economy.

Dr. Lee was a scholar in the Confucian tradition, and very thoughtful. During our first conversation he paused and asked me, "Do you think my people can learn?" This was a challenging question for a young consultant who had never been in Korea! I thought

---

for a minute, and then responded: "Well, it depends; do you believe they can learn?" He thought about this for several minutes and then responded, "Yes, I believe they can." I nodded, and we began our work together.

It was Dr. Lee's belief in his people's ability to learn and adapt that enabled him to launch a major and sustained effort to expand and deepen continuous learning across LG's organizations. It is this openness to continuous learning that enables organizations to succeed in the ever-changing conditions in the expanding global market.

LISTENING TO LEARN—DIALOGUE

Shared learning works best among people who are skilled in dialogue, which includes both the art of listening deeply to other people and the art of clearly explaining one's own thinking. To participate well in dialogue, we need to be open to sharing our ideas, our assumptions, and even our uncertainties. A colleague once told me he was hesitant to share his ideas in the group because they were "half-baked." I encouraged him to share his ideas with the group; in dialogue we would bake them together!

When we engage in dialogue, we seek to genuinely understand another person's (or group's) point of view. We also explain our own positions by letting others know what information we have used to arrive at our conclusions, and the way we interpret that information.

STORY: LISTENING TO LEARN

At Otis Elevator, conscious practice of this kind of dialogue had an impact throughout the organization. As Sandy Diehl, when he was Otis Elevator's vice president of

Marketing for North American Operations, reflected after his staff head had learned the use of dialogue, *"Now, people in meetings are conscious about whether they are listening to and learning from each other."*

As it undertook a major effort in organizational learning, Otis faced the challenge of gaining commitment from its field mechanics (those who repair and maintain Otis elevators) to new service standard procedures. To prepare for this I asked regional general managers to go out to the field mechanics and interview them, to learn the mechanics' thoughts about how to approach the managers' most pressing business problems. The Otis regional general managers came back impressed with the level of insight and information they received in their interviews with the field mechanics. When they approached their employees as learning partners, they found perceptions that were entirely new (and useful to them and the business).

They were so struck with the level of contribution that one regional general manager immediately put a field mechanic on his management committee. The president also made sure to check out the likely impacts of a new strategic initiative with a group of field mechanics before he launched it. Rather than give a prepared presentation, he held a meeting with the sole agenda of holding a dialogue and listening to feedback about the new initiative. As a result, he learned about organizational obstacles that had been invisible to senior management. Admitting his willingness to learn from others enabled him to create more effective strategies, and to build others' trust in him at the same time.

Barack Obama is quoted as saying that *"Respect means listening the most when you disagree the most!"* If we could all learn to do this, to listen rather than to jump in with our own opinions, we would be far more effective in all of our endeavors.

> **Reflection—Ask yourself:**
>
> Am I:
>
> - *Listening as if the person speaking is telling a truth that I really need to know?*
>
> - *Suspending my assumptions and listening to understand the other person's perceptions?*
>
> - *Appreciating the logic of the other person's viewpoint, even if it differs from my own logic?*

When you have engaged in dialogue in this way, you will understand better how others perceive the situation; you will be better able to align your thinking with others' in pursuit of results you both care about.

THE VALUE OF WRITING FOR REFLECTION

Reflective writing is an important learning skill that we can all use more effectively. Writing enables us to take random phenomena and organize them into coherent patterns. In other words, writing is thinking! This practice is especially useful when sorting out emotions or conflicting thoughts. Writing helps us locate the source of the thinking and interpretations that led to our conclusions. This reflection enables us to understand and transcend our initial reactions. I write whenever I want to understand something more deeply. I find this especially helpful when I am bothered by other people's actions or my response to them.

In the leadership programs I teach, after each experiential exercise, I always ask participants to write a few sentences in answer to the question "What have I learned?" Then I ask them to share their thoughts with someone else. This process of writing and sharing of reflections enables them to synthesize and make sense of what they are experiencing. They are able to draw lessons that they can apply when they lead others for results. Reflection is a key part of leadership development.

This is the continuous learning loop of action and reflection. Only through reflection can experience become knowledge that is useful for guiding future actions.

While skills such as dialogue, writing, and reflection are critically important in leading for results, they cannot fully contribute to a learning organization unless that organization demonstrates that it values learning. Many managers are trained to value action and speed; hence the "*ready, fire, aim*" mentality prevalent in so many organizations. Far too often, thinking is seen as a luxury, and collective thinking as a waste of time.

When you ask people to take time to learn together, you are asking them to unlearn some fundamental behaviors that they have used throughout their careers. This unlearning requires a shift in their basic assumptions. As a president of a national bank told me, after watching his senior managers engage in dialogue about key strategic issues, "*Sometimes you need to slow down to speed up.*"

Of course, the path from purpose and vision to results is rarely an entirely smooth one. You must expect to encounter obstacles, and even breakdowns. You may be able to see "true north" on the compass to direct you toward your destination, but remember there are oftentimes swamps and rivers to cross to get there.

LEADING THROUGH BREAKDOWNS

A *breakdown* is anything that stops the action or is in the way of achieving your result.

In taking on the responsibility of leading people, you will need to help your stakeholders understand how to approach breakdowns and find a way through that will result in new and better ways of doing things. You can use each breakdown on your path to realign your stakeholders around the common mission and move forward to achieve the results you want.

Even when you and your stakeholders are fully committed to achieving a result, you will continually be discovering what is missing and what is in the way of fulfilling your purpose. You may need to make corrections, both large and small, as you move toward your result. This is similar to "tacking" as you are sailing—you are always making corrections to reestablish the correct course.

STORY: BREAKDOWNS STOP PROGRESS TOWARD COMMITMENTS

I work with a small pharmaceutical company that is committed to delivering new and more effective cancer drugs. It was moving forward on launching a new drug. The manufacturing process was behind on delivering the needed materials to test that drug. This delay was perceived as a breakdown in the commitment of the company to deliver what it promised. There were a number of stakeholders, from internal team members to partner organizations to the board of directors and investors, all of whom had a stake in the success of this drug.

In order to get through the breakdown, they analyzed, without blame, what steps in the process needed more support, and which behaviors they needed to change to ensure adequate communications and alignment at every step of the process. By taking the time to analyze their breakdown, they not only got this drug back on track, they established better protocols for upcoming drugs as well.

Try to use each breakdown as a diagnostic opportunity that helps you understand what is missing or what stands in the way of achieving the results you desire.

Reflection—After a "breakdown" ask:

- *Have I clarified the result I am committed to accomplishing?*

- *Have I identified what was missing or gotten in the way of accomplishing that result?*

- *Do I see what actions are needed now to have a breakthrough?*

When others are involved:

- *Have I seen my role in the breakdown?*

- *Have I avoided blaming others?*

- *Have I communicated the breakdown in a timely way to engage the key stakeholders?*

Failure to handle breakdowns well can lead to minimizing or ignoring problems and blaming others, eroding both effectiveness and trust. When handled well, in contrast, breakdowns can be a major source of *breakthroughs*—new ways to approach your work and achieve results.

STORY: LEADING FROM BREAKDOWN TO BREAKTHROUGH

I worked at Lufthansa, in Frankfurt, Germany, with managers who were in the process of transforming functions such as food catering services to become independent business units, capable of selling to other airlines. The progress to make these changes was going slower than expected. As the managers worked together, they came to recognize that a top-down process, issuing orders or establishing new policies alone, was insufficient to achieve changes on the scale that was necessary.

The breakthrough for the Lufthansa managers came when they realized that their own beliefs about their employees would color how they designed their change process. At one point they held a heated debate among themselves about whether the people in their organizations were capable of change. One manager stated, "People here don't want to work very hard." Another senior manager countered with the evidence that the commitment of Lufthansa's employees had enabled the company to survive a massive restructuring and downsizing.

The exploration of the managers' beliefs about the employees and their capacity for change was a critical turning point. The managers in this dialogue arrived at a stronger appreciation for the workers in a massive organizational restructuring. They were able to move forward and design plans for communicating in a way that recognized and benefited from employees thinking about the restructuring process.

How our beliefs cause breakdowns

It is important to realize the limits of our own perceptions. Only 20 to 30 percent of our perceptions are actually determined by the information coming into us through our eyes, ears, and other senses. The fixed beliefs and models that already exist in our thinking shape our perceptions.

Creating assumptions or mental models is necessary for human survival. We need to order and classify our perceptions so that when we look at a wall, we know how to identify that in all of the figures we see there is a door to exit from. We know what a "chair" is from past beliefs and know we can sit in it. When people from primitive cultures who don't use chairs see a chair, they don't automatically know that this is something to sit on.

Children build up most of their models about how the world works before they are six years old. Our beliefs strongly affect and even *create* what we think we perceive. Very often it is actually the case that "believing is seeing." Since most of our beliefs are locked in before we have even reached adulthood, it's a wonder we can perceive new things at all!

Consequently, the first task in initiating shared learning is to create situations in which people feel safe enough to reveal their beliefs and assumptions. Only in this way can these be tested and validated. If we hold our beliefs to ourselves, we guarantee that we will become stuck in our own circular logic. We believe it, therefore we see evidence for it, and what we see confirms what we believe. The only way to begin to participate with others in shared learning is to begin sharing the beliefs and assumptions that we hold. Otherwise our perceptions will remain limited, incomplete, and inaccurate.

When I facilitate shared learning, I encourage people to listen carefully to the opinion that is most different from their own—the one that is seeing a radically different part of the reality. Only in this way can learning include all points of view to enable effective adaptation. The first question to ask yourself is "Am I willing to learn from this person?" If the answer to this is not authentically yes, it is a waste of time to continue acting as though you are in a genuine dialogue.

Authentic learning leads to effective adaptation, and adaptation is the key to the successful implementation of any project or program. There is a well-known saying: "Man plans and God laughs." I use this saying in leadership programs to emphasize the need for adaptation in the face of changing conditions. The military has a related saying: "No plan ever met a reality that couldn't defeat it."

When our own actions and behaviors create results that don't match our intentions, we need to be curious, and to reflect on what is missing and what we need to change. This continuous cycle of action and reflection is what enables us to synthesize our learning and use it to guide future actions. Every action that "fails" to accomplish our intended results contains within it an opportunity to learn—if we take that opportunity!

Learning is a transformation that takes place over time. It is the process by which we change the way we interpret or make sense of our experiences. We must first go through a period of awareness and acceptance of new information before we are able to act in new ways. Actions that we have reflected on—that is, examined and assessed—lead to new understandings, which in turn guide future actions.

Learning is most effective when we learn with others. When we learn together, we can share and build on one another's perceptions. As a result, we are able to hear other beliefs and test our own. This increases the likelihood of creating new interpretations that can guide more effective actions. When people learn in teams that exchange information rapidly and enjoy working together, they are better able to quickly correct mistaken ideas or procedures as they move toward results.

This doesn't mean that the process of shared learning is always a smooth one. As Peter Senge says: "Great teams are not characterized by a lack of conflict!"

Reflective writing

Buy a simple notebook and begin to write down your thoughts. Use this writing to examine what is behind your thoughts. Think about what beliefs you hold that lead you to your conclusions. Use the writing to clarify difficult emotions and thoughts, so that you are free to be present to new experiences with an open mind. To be most effective, get in the habit of examining your thoughts.

After each experience, ask yourself:

- *Is there something in my own thinking that is contributing to a situation I don't like?*

- *Is there some belief I need to test or change to move toward the results I want?*

- *What lessons can I take away from it that I can apply in the future?*

EXERCISE: HOLD A DIALOGUE WITH A CORE GROUP OF SUPPORTERS

Engage with a core group of supporters who understand your purpose and want to support you in accomplishing your result. This will be a small group at first, but if it is aligned around a shared vision, it will be strong and will expand.

Be sure to explain your own thoughts and underlying beliefs and assumptions openly.

And ask others:

- How do you envision the future of what we are working on?

- What thoughts do you have that are different than mine?

- What are the beliefs and assumptions that underlie your thinking?

When you have heard each other's thoughts, synthesize the best of all of your thinking and come to a common understanding.

EXERCISE: LEADING THROUGH BREAKDOWNS

This exercise is helpful when a group has experienced a breakdown and needs a process to resolve the issues effectively and without blame.

Call the group together to address the following questions:

- What result were we committed to accomplishing?

- What was missing that caused the breakdown to occur?

- What did you learn?

- What new actions could you take now?

- What support do you need to move forward to the result now?

By clarifying your commitments and the actions needed to fulfill on them, you lead the conversation in a positive forward direction.

Applying the Five Practices to the Personal Challenge of a Lifetime

The five practices described in *Leading for Results* have proven highly effective in helping people lead others to achieve the results they want in their organizations and communities. But they can also be used with great success to achieve results in your personal life. We are all, quite literally, leading our own lives. Here is a story from my own hard-won experience, to illustrate the use of the five practices in private life.

A few years ago I had a life-changing experience that gave me a prolonged and intense opportunity to clarify my purpose, envision a better future, frame a challenge, align many stakeholders, and do a lot of learning and adapting by questioning my own and others' beliefs.

In July 2007 I was in a plane crash in central Massachusetts. The four-seater Piper Cherokee in which I was a passenger crashed close to the end of the runway in a rural airport. The plane dropped down toward the end of the runway, then bounced back up and crashed into trees in a swamp some five hundred feet away. One wing broke off as the plane fell through the trees onto its side.

Emergency workers from several small towns arrived quickly and worked for over an hour to cut open the plane and evacuate the three people on board. They also had to cut through the deep growth in the surrounding swamp to evacuate us on stretchers. They took us by helicopter to an emergency trauma center at University of Massachusetts Memorial Hospital in Worcester. These rescue workers' committed actions saved all of our lives.

Prompt attention at the trauma center showed that I had suffered fourteen fractures, including three compression fractures to my lumbar spine. I was immediately put into emergency surgery to repair fractures in my left arm and elbow. I was also scheduled for exploratory surgery of my abdomen. Dr. Mansour, who is a surgeon from Egypt, accompanied me throughout the entire recovery process. He trusted his own manual exam over the inconclusive image revealed by the ultrasound technology. He insisted that the trauma surgeons wait to see whether or not the spots they had seen would expand over the next several hours before opening my abdomen. He challenged the assumptions of the Western doctors, who relied on the ultrasound technology. The spots didn't expand over the next ten hours. They turned out to be oxygen in the back of my lung, as Dr. Mansour had thought; and I was spared the misery of an invasive surgery on top of all my other difficulties.

I was transferred to the Spaulding Rehabilitation Hospital in Boston, where I was continuously challenged to learn how to use my body again. In the first hour after my arrival, a young physical therapist came to my bed and asked me to stand up. This seemed impossible to me, but he was a nice young man, and I wanted to cooperate. So I envisioned myself as an Apollo rocket on liftoff, and saw my legs as an enormous yellow-and-blue fire lifting me off. This imaging was the only way I could get off the bed for many weeks!

I was in physical therapy, occupational therapy, and speech

therapy every day. The staff provided the critical challenges and support I needed to learn how to adapt to my new situation. I came to respect them deeply for the care they provided and for their commitment to my recovery.

For three months I remained in a back brace as I slowly learned how to use all my limbs again. When my vertebrae finally (thankfully!) healed, the brace was removed. I will always remember the day when I learned that my spine would not be permanently damaged. Words cannot describe the relief.

I began a long course of recovery. My first exercises were moving my hand to regain use of my hands and both wrists, and walking up and down the length of the hall to build my stamina. I was making progress on my physical recovery, but seven months after the accident, I had the feeling that something was not right in my perceptions. I went to see a neurologist who diagnosed that I had what she called a "permanent mild traumatic brain injury." She said that there were hemorrhages on my brain that caused certain pathways not to work, causing symptoms such as slowness in word retrieval. She told me that my pain was linked to these brain injuries and that I probably would not be able to do "complex" work in the future. She recommended that I stop doing my work and handed me Social Security disability application forms!

As a management consultant, leadership teacher, and executive coach, I found this information more traumatic than the crash itself. I was angry and refused to accept this prognosis. Deep inside, however, I was badly hurt by it, and scared.

I was determined to find a way through this. I took it on as a challenge, envisioning a full recovery as my desired outcome and identifying the obstacles I had to overcome to achieve it. Even though the doctor had told me I could not write, I took on the challenge of writing an article about the leadership development program in Egypt. That article was accepted for publication in a

World Health Organization journal two years after my accident. Writing it proved to be the most effective therapy I could have undertaken. Writing forced me to think rigorously, as I synthesized my experiences from many years of creating and implementing the MSH Leadership Development Program.

The leadership curriculum that I had written was now expanding to many countries and needed editing and updating. With great support from colleagues, especially Jennifer Leonardo, the program manager from MSH, who came to my house in the evening and helped me to organize the work, I was able to edit and update the program.

What was going on in my brain was not all bad. I experienced a quietness that I came to appreciate. It helped me to be more present with my emotions and the emotions of others. It also gave me a kind of childlike wonder that I enjoyed. I learned how to trust my intuition more, and this has proven to be extremely effective in both teaching and coaching.

For more than two years I struggled with pain. I believe that the pain that persisted into the second year was a response to the prescription narcotics I was on for the first eight months of my recovery. When I was finished with those pain medicines, doctors prescribed both Ritalin and amphetamines to alleviate the pain and the slowness in my brain. I took each of these drugs for just one day before discarding them. I did not want to add more chemicals to my brain—especially since no one really understood how my brain was working or what the medications would do.

I believe that the healing of my pain was aided by the meditation that I did for an hour a day for a year. My Svaroopa yoga teachers, Swami Nirmalananda Saraswati and Deborah Shapiro, taught me how to meditate daily and do yogic breathing. This practice allowed the pain to gradually pass. I know that it helped because on the days when I did not meditate, the pain returned. Now, more than four years later, thankfully, I do not experience chronic pain, even in stressful situations such as international travel.

I began teaching again, but my speech was still slow. A year after I saw the neurologist who told me I had permanent brain damage, I decided to consult a behavioral neurologist, a doctor trained in both psychiatry and neurology. I waited several months for this appointment. This doctor asked me to take one more MRI of my brain before seeing him. I was hesitant to do so because at this point I found the experience of even setting foot in hospitals traumatic. Nonetheless, I did it—in tears. This was so unlike the "brave" demeanor that had been part of my former persona!

At the appointment, the behavioral neurologist told me, "I have good news. The MRI shows that you have no injuries in your brain." I was perplexed and asked, "How can that be when the first neurologist told me I had permanent brain damage?" He said, "Well, in 2009 we really didn't know that much about the brain."

This response from one of the leading neurologists in the world—admitting what he did not know—immediately won my trust and undying gratitude.

I then asked him, "Should I believe that I am all right?" And he said, "Yes. We find that what people believe has a big impact on their outcomes." (A doctor's rendition of "believing is seeing!") Finally I asked him, "Do I ever need to come back to the neurology clinic again?" And he said, "You are welcome to visit, but no, you never need to come to neurology again."

As I write this now, I cry for the relief I felt from his words. The very next day my speech hesitation disappeared. I realized that what had been happening was that every time I had trouble finding a word, I began to envision the blocked pathways that the first neurologist had described. Believing that the difficulty was due to a physical blockage slowed my speech.

This experience follows the paradoxical adage "We see what we believe." Once I had envisioned my brain as clear, even when I could not quickly retrieve a word, I just kept talking and the word came back to me. I came to understand that everyone has trouble with word retrieval from time to time, and I did not let this stop me from speaking smoothly.

Now I am again speaking at a normal pace. In the years since the accident I have taught students, managers, and executives around the world with great success. The legacy of the crash is still with me, but mostly in positive ways. For instance, I have retained the sensitivity that came from those years of being in recovery. I can feel my own and other people's suffering and emotions much more clearly than I did before the crash. I slow down to be with whatever is happening in the present, and I trust my own intuition much more. All this has greatly improved my ability to be with others in an empathetic way.

The long recovery from this accident was a huge learning experience that took place over several years. There were so many challenges that required me to learn from experience. Here are just a few of them:

After a year of physical therapy, I was told that I would never have full mobility in my left shoulder. I refused to accept this outcome; instead, I researched and found specialized myofascial therapists who released the scar tissue (a painful process that took many months) and enabled me to get back full mobility of my arm.

I was told that the double vision I was experiencing could not be corrected by therapy and would require surgery. But I found eye therapists who helped me learn how to retrain my vision. At every turn I had to envision health, and to seek the actions that would lead toward the results I wanted.

While I faced challenges, I also had support. I had many trusted advisors with whom I spoke regularly; they helped me reflect on and understand the many emotions that accompanied these changes. I wanted to be whole and complete, not just in my body, but also in my mind and emotions. I did not want to carry any remains of this trauma. I wanted to be able to put the past in the past so that I could be present to experience the beauty of today. (As I write this, it's quite a stunning early November day in New England.) To do this work, I needed to trust people and share even my darkest thoughts, so that I could emerge again whole and complete and able to participate and contribute fully in the world.

The *Leading for Results* practices proved invaluable in my own transformation back to good health:

- *I clarified my purpose and recommitted myself to being a fully contributing professional who consults, teaches, and writes in the field of leadership development.*

- *I envisioned the results I wanted: to be a "healthy old lady." Toward this end, I compiled a collection of photographs of healthy old women, which I look at every day.*

- *I framed challenge after challenge, and have worked continuously toward achieving measurable results, including regaining fluent speech, clear vision, full mobility, and a fit body.*

- *I aligned my stakeholders, including friends, family members, colleagues, medical practitioners, and therapists from several disciplines, to help me make progress toward the results I wanted.*

- *I learned and adapted every day, finding new ways to accomplish the results that were important to me. I found a gym and trainer, Greatest Age Fitness in West Newton,*

Massachusetts, founded by Mo Lanier, that specializes in working with people to adapt and be fit as we age. I am a lifelong learner of new ways to strengthen my agility and balance.

Before the crash I had wanted to slow down, to have more time to reflect. In fact, I had written in my journal, "I want to strengthen my abilities to bring coherence to my thoughts and experiences. I want to take time to make sense out of the many experiences I have had in my life. I need to carve out time to reflect productively, to strengthen my understanding of my life's work."

I now include reflection in my daily life. I don't need to experience traumatic events to recognize the importance of reflection. But I have learned that in the face of change, especially in times of trauma or loss, it is important to use the reflective practices to learn, adapt, and grow. Writing this book has called on me to reflect and to bring coherence to my thoughts and experiences over the course of my career in leadership development.

I am grateful to be alive and fully functioning today. I discovered that I needed to trust myself and other wise people to guide me through what I needed to learn. And I am thrilled to say that I adapted and grew and will continue to until the day I die.

Afterword:
How I Became Committed
to Teaching Leadership

My path to becoming a teacher of leadership began in childhood. As a child, I observed my father, who was the founder and president of a successful engineering firm. He was also a leader of religious and charitable organizations in our community. I learned his approach to leading by watching the respectful yet purposeful way that he interacted with his colleagues and employees.

He explained to me that to work effectively with people you first need to make clear the answer to the question, "What are we really trying to do here?" He also encouraged me to find my own purpose in life, saying, "When you do what you love, you do it well." Most important, he shared with me what he had learned as a young naval officer in World War II: "You don't *manage* people; you *lead* them."

Another source of inspiration was watching my mother's life as it evolved in the 1960s. Once my brother and I were both in school, she returned to college, stretching herself beyond the roles of wife and mother. Every evening of my childhood, I watched her studying. She received her college degree when she was 42 years old and went on to become a professional counselor, supporting others to fulfill their aspirations. She always encouraged me to make the largest contribution possible.

I came of age in New York City in the early 1970s, a time when the possibilities for women's lives were in rapid transition. The structure of my own family was also in transition as my mother moved out into the workforce. I found a way to have a voice in these changes through teaching and speaking in films about the many choices young women were facing. In my senior year in high school, I summarized what I was learning in an essay that I wrote out by hand with a ballpoint pen and sent off to Harvard University. Much to my surprise, I was accepted there as a freshman in the fall of 1972.

At Harvard I focused my studies on subjects that I thought might help me to understand the vast economic and social changes I saw around me. I sensed that the family and women's health issues that I cared about were linked to the larger changes underway in society, and wanted to understand how these economic and social forces were shaping our lives.

After graduating from Harvard, I sought first-hand understanding of the lives of people working at the base of our industrial society. So I went to work in Quincy Shipyard, where I spent five years as a welder, working with some 5,000 other laborers, outdoors, on steel, in all seasons. I always say, only partly jokingly, that I learned more in the shipyard than I learned at Harvard. Most important, I learned there how to listen to and learn from the experiences of others.

During this period I married and had two children. In the course of my first pregnancy, I applied to obtain the medical leave benefits due me, and found out that clauses in the union contract specifically cited pregnancy as the one medical condition the company did not need to compensate for. In the process of trying to obtain my own rights, I found myself in the leadership of a two-year campaign to win maternity benefits for pregnant workers.

In the course of this campaign we aligned 800 mostly male shipyard workers to sign a petition supporting women's maternity benefits. Even older male shipyard workers whose wives had stayed home to raise their children supported us. I remember one older worker with a stay-at-home wife who at first objected to what we were doing, but then thought about it and said, *"I don't know how you young people survive the way prices are today. You do need two people to work. I will sign that petition!"* From this experience I learned how to align a diverse group of stakeholders around a common purpose and vision.

After my second child was born, I left the shipyard and went to work part-time as a community educator for a local family planning agency. There I organized a troupe of teenaged mothers to educate other teenagers about the realities of teen pregnancy and motherhood. This program had an impact on both the audiences and the teen mothers themselves, for whom it offered validation of their life experiences and the opportunity to contribute to others.

To make sense of these experiences and broaden my capabilities, I enrolled in Harvard's Graduate School of Education. I also took courses at the Kennedy School of Government, where I was drawn strongly to the subject of leadership. Working with Professor Ronald Heifetz, I learned about "leading without authority," an idea that resonated deeply with much of my own experience. It was in his course that I first formulated my life's purpose as "teaching leadership."

In the course of earning my doctorate, I worked in the research department of The Forum Corporation, a global training firm. There I conducted research on the leadership practices of high-performing managers in multinational business firms. This research formed the basis of my Harvard doctoral dissertation. I have used the leadership practices that I identified in the course of this research as the foundation for the leadership development programs I have designed and taught in the business and public sectors.

For a dozen years I worked in the business world. I was a consultant, manager, and director in high-powered, innovative consulting companies, including Arthur D. Little, Inc. and Innovation Associates, Inc. This phase of my career constituted a fast-paced apprenticeship with some of the outstanding pioneers and teachers in the field of leadership development and organizational learning, including Peter Senge. I learned how to teach leadership to managers and executives in multinational organizations across North America, Asia, and Europe.

In 2000 I was asked to take up the challenge of bringing the lessons I had learned in leadership development in the business sector to Management Sciences for Health (MSH). MSH is a global public health organization committed to improving health systems in the poorest countries. As part of a USAID-funded project, I worked with dedicated people from the U.S. and from countries in Latin America, Africa, and the Middle East to develop the MSH Leadership Development Program (LDP).

The LDP, a six month long program that supports health teams to lead for results, further validated the leadership practices by testing them in a wide range of cultures to ensure that they could be easily understood and applied anywhere by anyone. It used the best thinking in experiential adult learning to create an effective program that has been delivered in more than 40 countries --- empowering thousands of health managers and their teams to improve health results for those most in need. I was the lead author of <u>Managers who Lead,</u> a book published by MSH in

2005. Health managers around the world use this book to guide them in achieving improvements in health services.

The *Leading for Results* practices presented in this book are the outgrowth of all these experiences. Today I work in both the private and the public sectors with high performers who are committed to making a difference. I teach leadership programs in organizations and at universities. I coach individuals and teams to face challenges and achieve results. It has been a joy to be able to live out my purpose: teaching leadership.

I hope you will benefit from *Leading for Results*. Please write to me at joan@bostonleadership.com and tell me what you have learned by applying these practices. You can also find more information at my website: www.bostonleadership.com.

Your Personal *Leading for Results* Checklist

The practices in this book can help guide your day-to-day actions as you move toward achieving your goals.

Review the questions below to see where you are in your own process of leading for results.

- Have I clarified my purpose in a way that gives meaning to my work and life?
- Have I created an inspiring vision of a future I want to work toward?
- Have I identified a measurable result that I could achieve in the next six months that would bring me closer to that vision?
- Have I framed the challenge as a question? *"How can I achieve this result in the face of these obstacles?"*
- Have I identified my key stakeholders, and do I understand their needs and concerns?
- Have I communicated requests to stakeholders for resources I need?
- Do I fully and frequently acknowledge the contributions of others?
- Have I made time to reflect and learn so that I can adapt and grow as needed?

CPSIA information can be obtained
at www.ICGtesting.com
Printed in the USA
LVOW11s2245070717
540604LV00001B/2/P